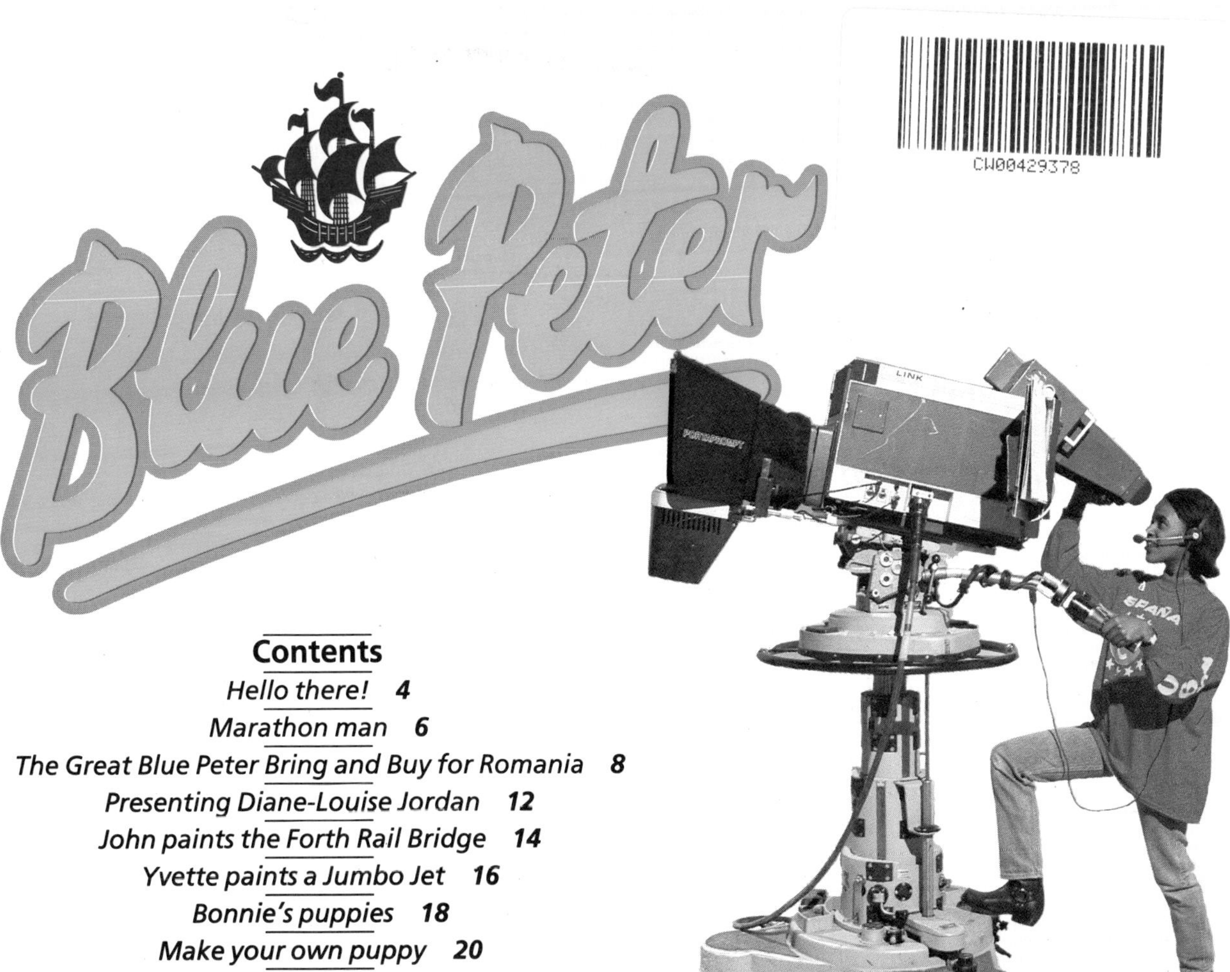

Contents

BOOK 26

Written by Lewis Bronze and John Comerford
Co-ordinated by Anne Dixon

£4.50

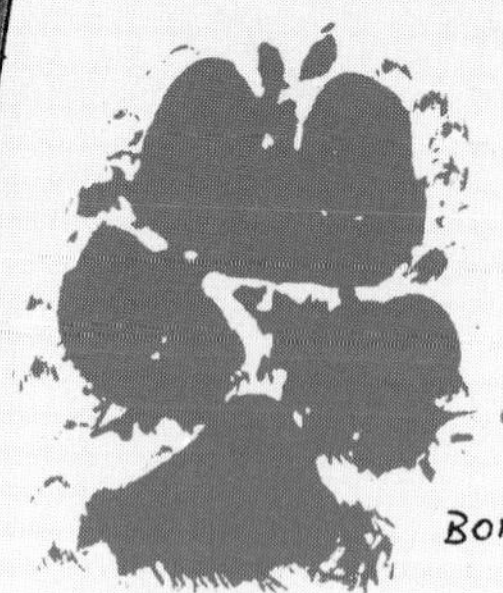

Hello

BONNIE

WILLOW

Welcome aboard Blue Peter's twenty-sixth annual! We can promise you lots of good stories and plenty of fun pictures over the next sixty pages, so eyes down for a meaty read!

1991 has been a remarkable year for everyone on Blue Peter, even by the high standards of the programme. It began with the most successful appeal we've ever run – the Great Blue Peter Bring and Buy for Romania. The highlights of this marvellous appeal are on pages 8–11, including pictures from Yvette's reports from Romania.

And John's been pretty busy too! In the winter and spring he was pounding the pavements in a bid to take part in the ADT London Marathon – find out how he did on page 6.

As for Diane, she's hardly stopped since the day she joined Blue Peter. You can go behind the scenes during the first nerve-racking day on page 44. Last winter she was in Norway,

△ Let's get that Greenhouse Effect! John and "Snoopy", the aeroplane that probes the atmosphere to measure pollution.

△ Paintbrush in paw, helping to get Montserrat straight after Hurricane Hugo.

▽ The oddest game of snooker ever seen on television. Diane demonstrates the flatness of a studio floor by potting the black. Don't think she'll worry Stephen Hendry!

◁ Under a threatening tropical sky, John and Diane try a spot of jet-skiing before the next downpour!

there!

John Leslie

HONEY

Diane-Louise Jordan

GEORGE

walking up a frozen waterfall. She also plunged into an icy snowhole – something she's not planning to repeat!

Bonnie also helped make 1991 special. She produced six lovely puppies in January. They are all in the middle of their guide dog training – we'll have more news of them during 1992. Honey, the puppy being walked by John, is already something of a star. She has a lively personality and is a natural on television!

You can get some idea of what a great year it has been just from the pictures on these pages. How many of them can you remember?

We hope you enjoy our adventures and getting to know us through reading our profile pages – don't miss the puzzles on Yvette's and John's pages. And don't forget you can keep up with all the Blue Peter happenings every Monday and Thursday on Children's BBC – it won't be the same without you!

◁ Yvette with world-champion rally driver Louise Aitken-Walker. "The most exciting thing I've yet done on Blue Peter!" says Yvette.

▽ How do you change a lightbulb in a TV studio? Diane wonders if someone's been winding her up!

△ Who's been sitting in Magnus's chair? Yvette tries it for size but doesn't expect to win Mastermind next year!

△ The most valuable item ever seen on Blue Peter. No, not the one on the left! The suit of armour belonged to King Henry VIII and is worth eleven million pounds!

◁ Bernard Cribbins has read a hundred stories on Jackanory. He joined Diane for a celebration of the programme's twenty-fifth birthday.

MARATHON MAN

John's the kind of guy who's slow to turn down any kind of sporting challenge. So when world-famous runner Steve Cram offered to coach him for the London Marathon, there was no question! But this particular challenge demanded a little more than just sheer enthusiasm . . .

A wintry day at Steve's running club in Jarrow began with warm-ups, followed by an endless jog around the shipyards of Tyneside and on to the hills and dales of Northumberland, and a lecture on diet and exercise. John began to wonder if he'd bitten off more than he could chew.

John was a familiar figure pounding the streets of south-west London over the next few weeks, desperately trying to keep to his running target of fifty miles a week.

◁ **John trained for the marathon under the care of World Champion runner Steve Cram.**

▽ **While Steve tucked into pie and chips, John stuck to a healthier lunch!**

LON

ST PAUL'S
TRAFALGAR SQUARE
BUCKINGHAM PALACE
BIG BEN
FINISH
TOWER BRIDGE
WESTMINSTER BRIDGE

THE ROUTE
26 MILES

8.30 am: 21st April 1991, Blackheath, London. Marathon day. The sun's shining and 23,000 runners young and old, of every shape and size, are getting ready. Among them is a nervous TV presenter. He hasn't slept. He doesn't know if he can do it. Too late for any more preparation – just time for last minute tips from marathon veteran Peter Duncan and hasty Vaseline applications to stop rubbing.

9.30 am: The cannon sounds and the 1991 ADT London Marathon is underway. A human wave spills on to the streets of London for the 26-mile course. Runner 14712 soon finds his pace – at the eleven-mile stage he looks strong and confident and is making good time. But the worst is yet to come.

11.20 am: Tower Bridge. Thirteen miles. Diane offers words of encouragement and John heads for the toughest stretch through Docklands. Surrounded by Andy Pandy, Snow White and the Seven Dwarfs and a bright green parrot, John is travelling light, but the huge distance is taking its toll on Leslie's long legs.

Sheer determination carried hobbling John over Westminster Bridge and on to the finishing line in a respectable 4 hours 42 minutes. He had just enough energy to grab a sandwich as a marathon official wrapped a foil blanket round his shoulders.

Later, proud of his achievement, he said: "Running a marathon must be one of the toughest things a human can do – no machinery to help, just you, your two legs and a load of will-power. And I'll *never* do it again!"

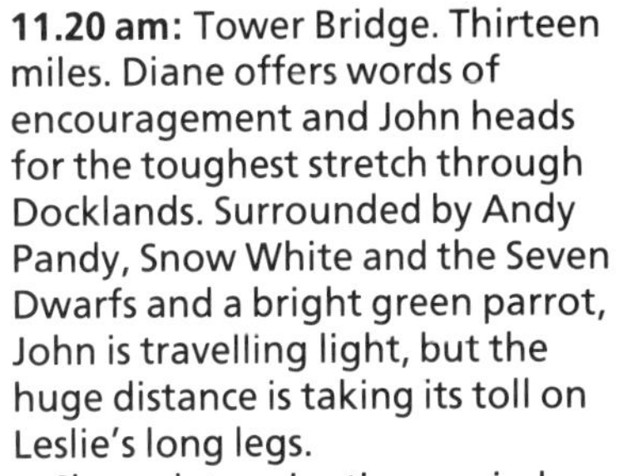

◁ **At last! The only time John will ever cross the finish line in a marathon!**

The Great Blue Peter Bring & Buy for ROMANIA

If there's a more generous group of people than the viewers of Blue Peter, we've yet to hear of them. For the 1990 Blue Peter Appeal, our viewers did more than ever before. It was all to help children in another country who had never heard of Britain, and who never believed such kindness existed in the world.

The children you helped are the thousands who lived in utter squalor in the forgotten orphanages of Romania. For years the orphanages were one of Romania's darkest secrets – dustbins for humans, places to leave unwanted children whose parents had no hope of caring for them in a country where food, housing, fuel and clothes are in desperately short supply.

There was a revolution in Romania in 1989. That's when the secret orphanages became known to the outside world. The awful pictures of children thumping their heads against the metal bars of their cots out of sheer boredom looked more like animals in a zoo than babies in a nursery.

▷ *The orphanage laundry was typical of many – rusty, broken machines unable to cope with the workload.*

▷ *While he crammed the orphanages full of unwanted children, Ceausescu built himself the biggest palace in the world.*

▷ *Someone seems very interested in our cameraman's trouser pocket! In the foreground, you can see one of the play rings, shown in the studio, being used in the Piâtre Neamt orphanage.*

Blue Peter got involved thanks to a remarkable lady called Mary Gibson. Mary saw the pictures on the TV news and went out to Romania with the aim of doing something to help the children. She set up the Romanian Orphanage Trust and began finding small teams of nannies and nurses to go and work in the orphanages alongside the Romanian staff.

The Trust, like many British groups, began sending lorryloads of things to the orphanages – toys, clothes, nappies – but Mary realized that while those items were badly needed, they did not provide a long-term answer to the problems of the children living in such awful conditions.

We launched our 1990 Appeal with what might turn out to be an answer – a plan to build small, family-style homes in Romania for children from orphanages. To raise the money, we asked viewers to run their own Bring and Buys as they have done so successfully in the past. And to help the children during the many months needed to plan and build the houses, we also wanted to buy equipment for the orphanages.

Nobody on Blue Peter predicted the massive response we had as soon as the Appeal was launched. After just two days, thousands more Bring and Buy kits were being printed to cope with the demand. In a few days, the number of requests for kits

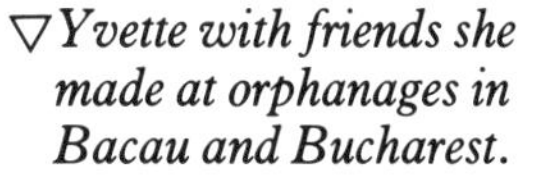

▽ *Yvette with friends she made at orphanages in Bacau and Bucharest.*

The Great *Blue Peter* Bring & Buy for ROMANIA

passed the record from previous Bring and Buy Appeals – and the number kept on growing.

By mid-November we knew Bring and Buys were planned for every city, town and village in Britain. The map we showed in the studio became so full of pins that we had to invent a new system – one gold pin to equal one hundred Bring and Buys.

Letters, photos, newspaper reports and videos kept arriving, and we tried to show as many as possible on our Appeal Noticeboard. The letters were the best of all. Through them we realized how much people really wanted to help the children in Romania.

By December 6th 1990, our first target of £625,000 had been passed. We raised it to £2,000,000, easily the largest amount of money we've ever asked Blue Peter viewers to raise. The extra sum would pay for more equipment for more orphanages, but most importantly, for training. Equipment alone – vital though it is – cannot improve the lives of children in orphanages in the long-term. Things will only really get better if the Romanian staff learn modern methods of childcare and understand that it can be much more rewarding to play with and stimulate a child than to treat it as an animal.

To do the training the Trust began to recruit teams from the charity Voluntary Service Overseas. A lot of the extra money was planned to pay for those teams to work in Romania throughout 1991. Another plan that was developed in consultation with the Romanian authorities was the opening of a college to teach young Romanian girls to the same standard as the British Nursery Nurse Education Board qualification. No such course existed before in Romania. The fact that one does now is due largely to Blue Peter viewers.

On Yvette's second visit to Romania, she went to an orphanage at a town called Piâtre Neamt that had received virtually no aid at all. She asked the Director if anything was needed, and the Director pulled a shopping list out of her pocket! On it were all kinds of machinery – washing machines, dryers,

▷ Two million pounds raised – and our first team of volunteers ready to set off to help the children in the Piâtre Neamt orphanage.

◁ At our celebrity Bring and Buy, Phillip and Gordon helped to raise money – but the Gopher wasn't for sale!

Garages are great places for Bring and Buys! Olivia Kenyon held her sale in her Grandma's in Wigan and raised £235.

Nine-year-old Carolyn Brown and her friends, from Shirley in the West Midlands, raised £55.69.

▷ *Maggie Kelly (far left) and John (right) of Barnardo's are working with Romanian staff to select the children who will live in the Blue Peter houses.*

kitchen stoves, cupboards, and much more.

On January 4th 1991, all that equipment was on display in the studio – all bound for the orphanage at Piâtre Neamt. Blue Peter viewers had reached £2 million – and there was no sign of the Appeal ending there!

Over the next few months, the money continued to pour in as more people held their Bring and Buys. The huge sum of £2,000,000 was left behind. We passed £3 million, then £4 million, then £5 million! By the beginning of May 1991, the Great Blue Peter Bring and Buy for Romania had raised £6,130,394.86!

In the meantime work was continuing in Romania. The hard winter frosts made it difficult to do much building, but once the spring came the first three houses quickly took shape in the town of Bacau, about 300 kilometres north of the capital, Bucharest. Blue Peter cameras filmed the houses ready for their first arrivals in May. The children lucky enough to live in them will be carefully selected by the Trust and the Romanian orphanage staff. They will come from all backgrounds. Some will be very ill, some will grow to become healthy people who we hope will play a full part in rebuilding their shattered country.

What is difficult for us in Britain to understand is that the tragedy of the Romanian orphanages is a man-made one. In fact, it was made by just one man, Nicolae Ceausescu, the President who was deposed and then executed in 1989. It was his policy that forced women to have five children. Once Ceausescu went, the numbers of babies being sent to orphanages dropped dramatically. In other words, this is a problem that might, one day, actually go away. Unlike famine in Africa, it might be ended.

The work will take many years, there will be many difficulties along the way – especially because Romania itself has not ended its political problems just by removing Ceausescu. But one day children in Romania might remember that what Blue Peter viewers – the children of Britain – did for them proved there is kindness in the world.

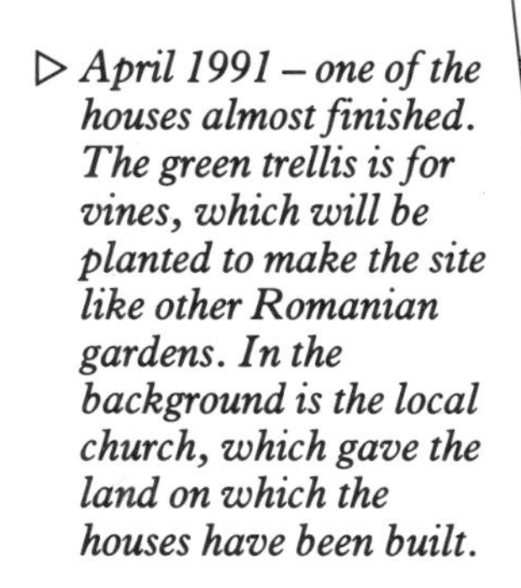

▷ *April 1991 – one of the houses almost finished. The green trellis is for vines, which will be planted to make the site like other Romanian gardens. In the background is the local church, which gave the land on which the houses have been built.*

Presenting Diane-Louise

No question about Diane's top adventure so far on Blue Peter – the 1990 Summer Expedition to the Caribbean. "I loved the weather, the people, the food, the music – everything!" she says.

"Another highlight was meeting the reggae band Aswad. They came to the studio before we went and then we met them again when we filmed at Reggae Sunsplash in Jamaica – they were great!"

Diane really loves being on Blue Peter. "The variety of places we visit and things we do is wonderful. I remember one week when, after Monday's programme, I flew to the North-east, went swimming with a dolphin and filmed on a fishing boat, flew back to London for Thursday's studio, then went off to film woolly monkeys in Cornwall on Friday. I'd been dreading that week, but it was just great, and while I had woolly monkeys jumping all over me, I thought how lucky I was to be on Blue Peter!"

Two-year-old Diane-Louise with big sister Jay.

Jordan

FACTFILE

Born: Hackney
Birthday: 27 February
School: Hatfield Comprehensive
Qualifications: 5 O Levels, 1 O/A Level, 2 A Levels , B A (Hons) in Theatre Arts.
Best subject: History, English, Drama
Worst subject: Maths
Pets: Lucky, a very old imitation Border Collie
Fave group: Dennis Brown, Aswad
Fave actor: Robert de Niro
Fave actress: Pamela Nomvete (from Eastenders), Miranda Richardson
Fave film: Great Expectations (with Michael York)
Fave sport: Running, gymnastics, ice-skating
Fave TV series: Blue Peter (of course!)
Person I most admire: My Mum
Car: Honda Civic (and a damaged Morris Minor)
Fave food: Chocolate
Least fave food: Curry
Fave ice-cream: Chocolate
Thing I hate most in all the world: Cooking
Fave country: Dominica
Things I always have on me: (I never have the things I need) old receipts and dirty tissues
Fave book: Touching the Void by Joe Simpson
Fave book when younger : the Borrowers by Mary Norton

Diane and the class of 1980 at the Rose Bruford College of Speech and Drama.

John paints the FORTH RAIL BRIDGE

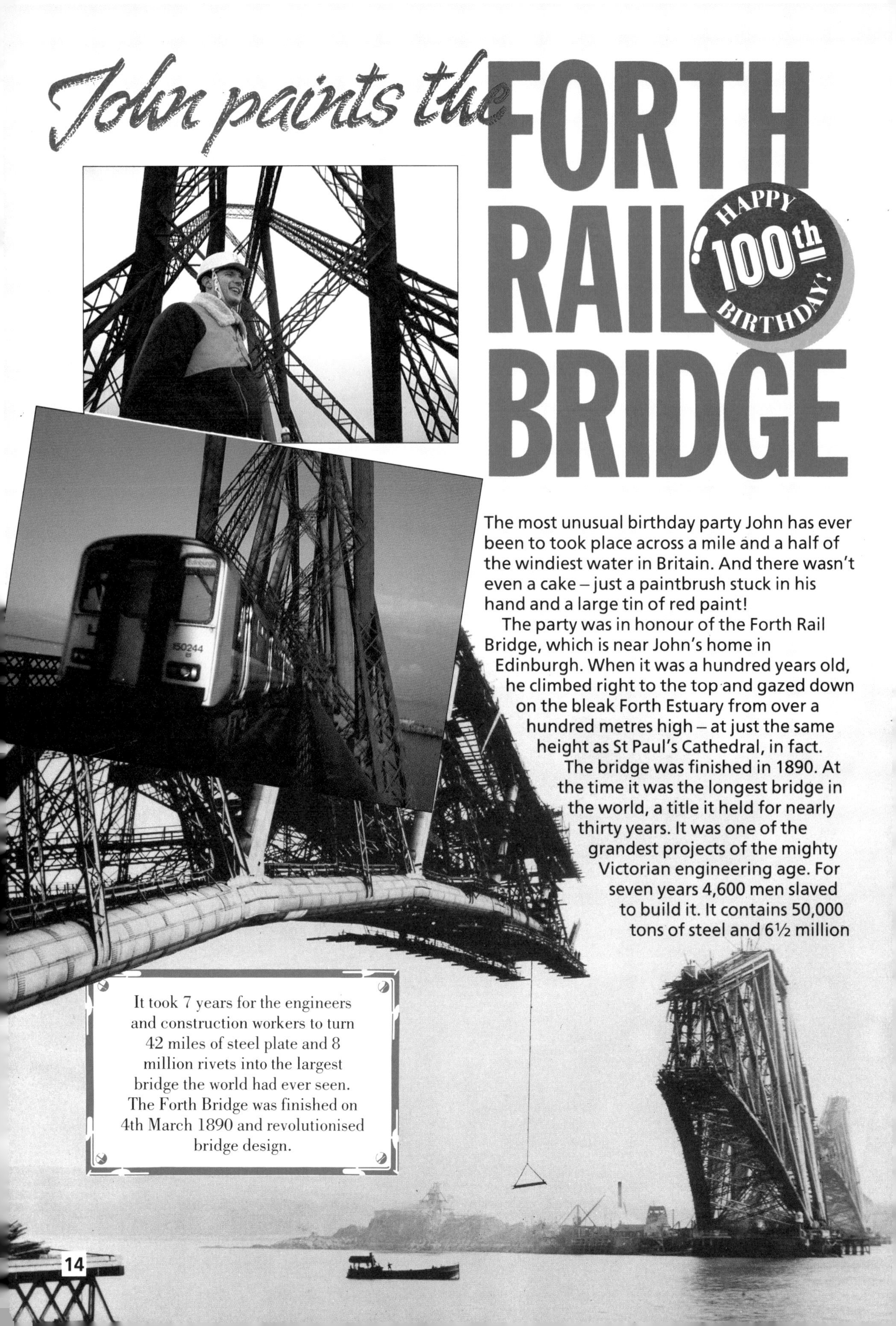

The most unusual birthday party John has ever been to took place across a mile and a half of the windiest water in Britain. And there wasn't even a cake – just a paintbrush stuck in his hand and a large tin of red paint!

The party was in honour of the Forth Rail Bridge, which is near John's home in Edinburgh. When it was a hundred years old, he climbed right to the top and gazed down on the bleak Forth Estuary from over a hundred metres high – at just the same height as St Paul's Cathedral, in fact.

The bridge was finished in 1890. At the time it was the longest bridge in the world, a title it held for nearly thirty years. It was one of the grandest projects of the mighty Victorian engineering age. For seven years 4,600 men slaved to build it. It contains 50,000 tons of steel and 6½ million

It took 7 years for the engineers and construction workers to turn 42 miles of steel plate and 8 million rivets into the largest bridge the world had ever seen. The Forth Bridge was finished on 4th March 1890 and revolutionised bridge design.

△Hidden among the girders is the painters' tea room!

◁John sets off bravely for the top.

rivets – all put together so well that not a single girder has ever been replaced!

Painting the bridge really is a never-ending job. John discovered that it takes about five years to do the whole structure, and, yes, as soon as they've finished, they start again! They use a specially formulated paint called "Forth Bridge Red", designed to stand up to the incredible battering of salt, spray and wind. Not only do the painters need a good head for heights, they have to get used to express trains thundering past only a few metres away.

The bridge has a secret – a little hut wedged up in the structure hides a canteen for the painters. They don't have to go far for a cuppa! If you're ever in a train going over the Forth Rail Bridge, try looking up – you may be lucky enough to spot the oddest tea room in Scotland!

Yvette paints a JUMBO JET

Eighty thousand pounds might sound like a lot of money for sitting around doing nothing – but that's what it costs British Airways to keep just one of its fleet of fifty Jumbos on the ground for a day.

That's why, when Golf-Alpha-Whisky-November-Michael rolled into a special hangar at Heathrow Airport for a major face lift, every second counted!

Yvette put on her painting overalls and joined the thirty-man team responsible for putting the shine back on to the fading 747. Twelve days were timetabled for the transformation and not a moment longer. The pressure was on.

The first task was to position acres of masking to protect the windows and sensitive areas of this vast metal bird from chemicals and paint.

For the second stage it was on with a space-age suit and breathing equipment. You don't take chances when four hundred gallons of chemical are being sprayed about, capable of stripping the aircraft down to the bare metal.

It's not just a cosmetic job – once stripped, the exposed aircraft is carefully examined for signs of

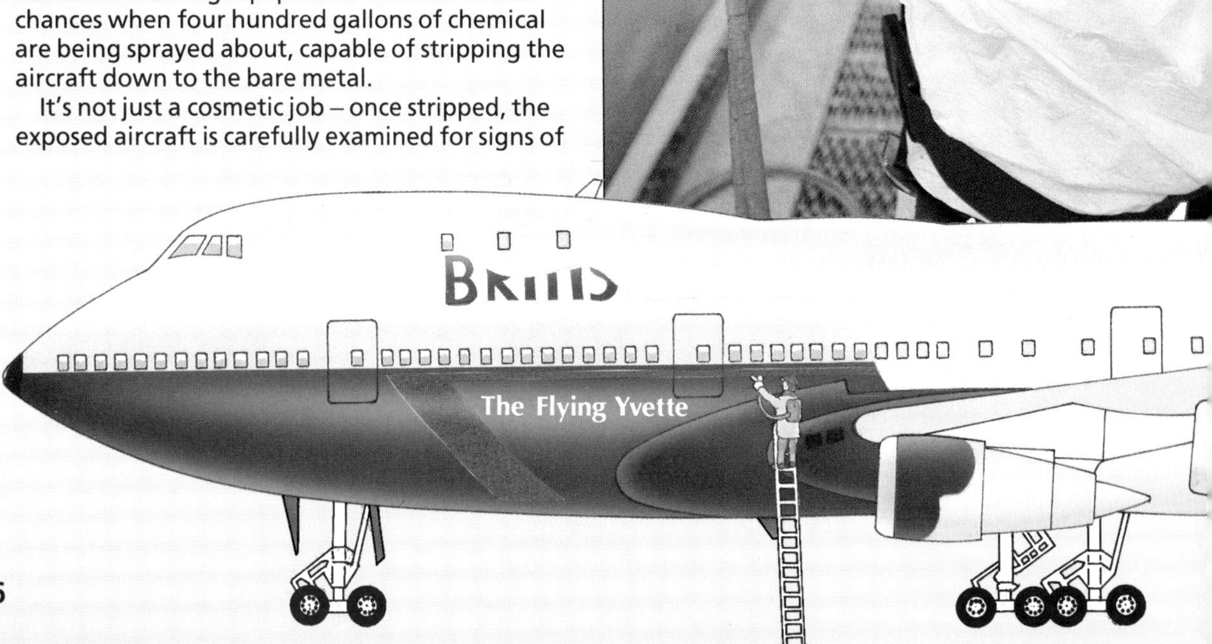

wear and tear; and when it's all finished, smooth and shiny, it actually saves money on fuel!

The fun starts with the paint guns – pearl grey on the top and deep midnight blue on the bottom. The finishing touch – a distinctive red speed stripe down the side. "It's quite an art to get it right," Yvette claimed. "Light, even strokes are the answer – too much and you're adding extra weight to the aircraft, too little and it looks patchy."

The now-gleaming November-Mike needed only one final finishing touch. Fielding stepped forward without a moment's hesitation and left her mark – *The Flying Yvette*.

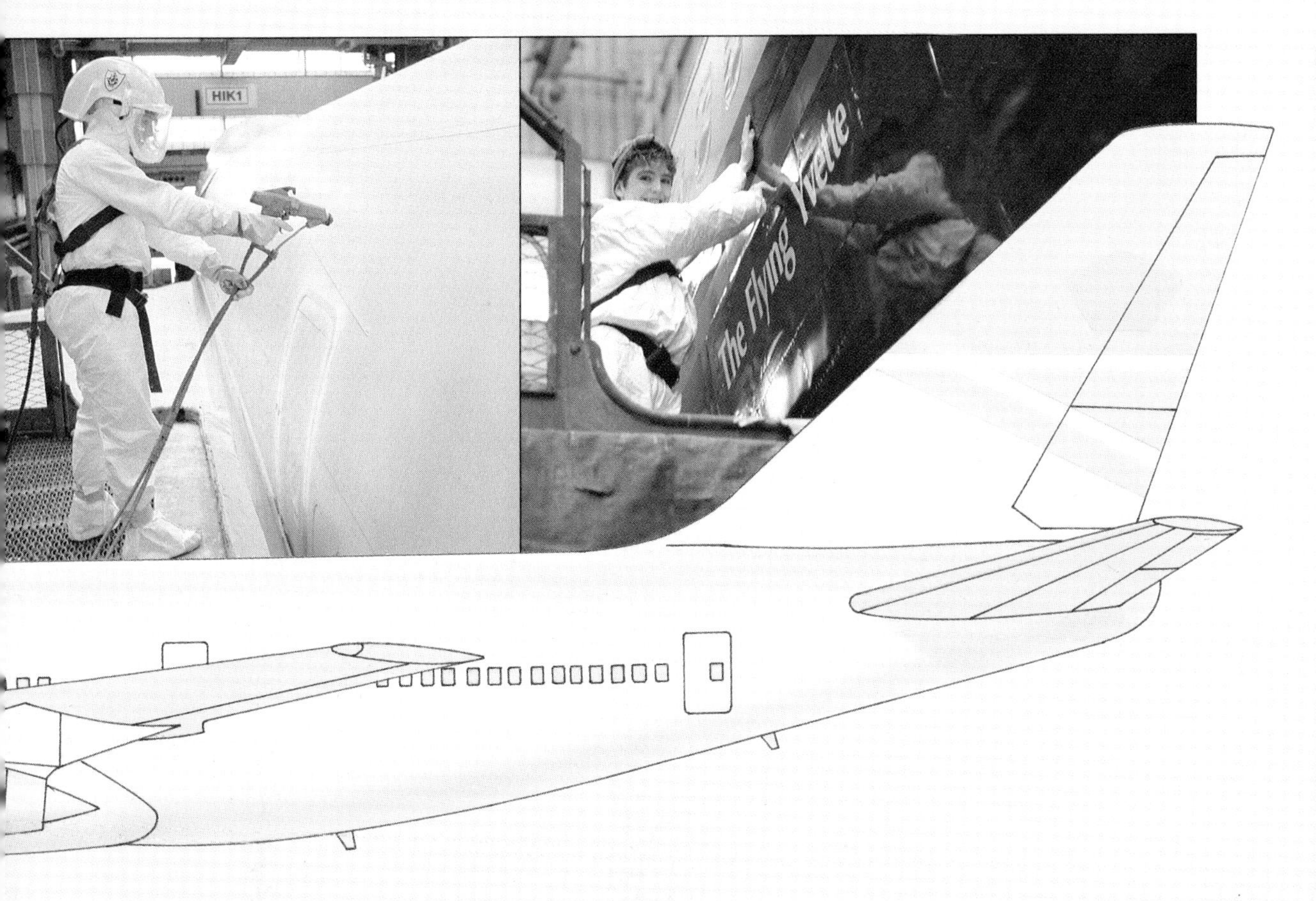

Bonnie's Puppies

Six little bundles of happiness came into Blue Peter's world on 16th January 1991, when our favourite Golden Retriever had her litter of puppies. Bonnie is the best – and she's got her six pups to prove it!

The puppies were born quite quickly, starting in the middle of the night. Leonie Pocock, who looks after Bonnie, carefully weighed each one. There was a seventh, very small puppy. "He was hardly breathing, so I gave him the kiss of life by blowing gently into his mouth," said Leonie. Sadly, the seventh did not make it, which is not unusual in litters of this size.

Bonnie is a great mum, and her pups soon put on weight. After ten days, they were eating chopped mince and cereal. When they were exactly six weeks old, Leonie piled them all in the car and

off they went to the studio. They are true television stars – happily sleeping in their special pen when they were not in front of the cameras. Once the programme began, they played, sniffed and generally explored everything in sight!

Forty-five thousand suggestions were made by Blue Peter viewers for the puppies' names. Finally, we settled on our six favourites: Major (after the new Prime Minister), Margot (after Dame Margot Fonteyn), Biddy (after Biddy Baxter, who ran Blue Peter for twenty-seven years), Lily, Teddy and Honey. Honey was the name of Blue Peter's very first guide dog puppy in 1965.

Honey's progress is being followed by Blue Peter because John and Leonie are in charge of her puppy walking – that's her training to be a guide dog. Honey's first walk with John was on 9th April. She met geese in Kew Gardens, saw a train, went on a river boat and did not panic in front of heavy London traffic. She behaved beautifully!

Make your own Puppy

This has to be the Blue Peter make of this and many a year! These little puppies are so adorable, you'll just have to have one. Who would ever dream they started life as a fabric conditioner bottle?!

You will need

2-litre fabric conditioner bottle (empty and cleaned out)
fawn-coloured knitting wool
rubber solution or clear glue
fawn-coloured felt or brown paper
1 black button (with shank)
2 black beads
a scrap of pink felt or paper

1. Mark a point 14.5 cm from the top of the bottle. Draw a sloping line up to the other side. The line goes through the gap in the handle. Cut across the line – you may need some help.

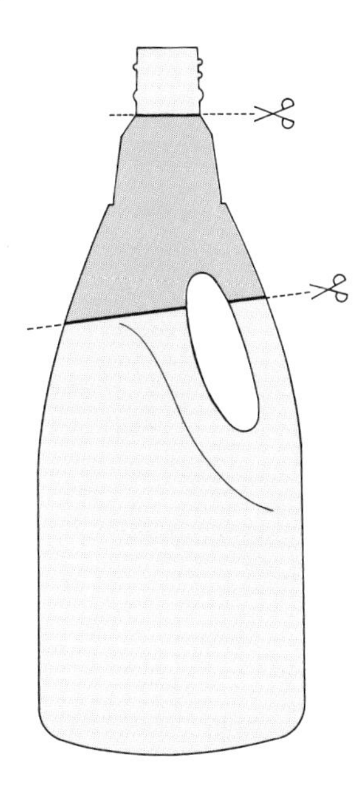

2. Wind the wool around four fingers about ten times. Carefully cut through the loops to make strands. Snip off pieces 0.5 cm long.

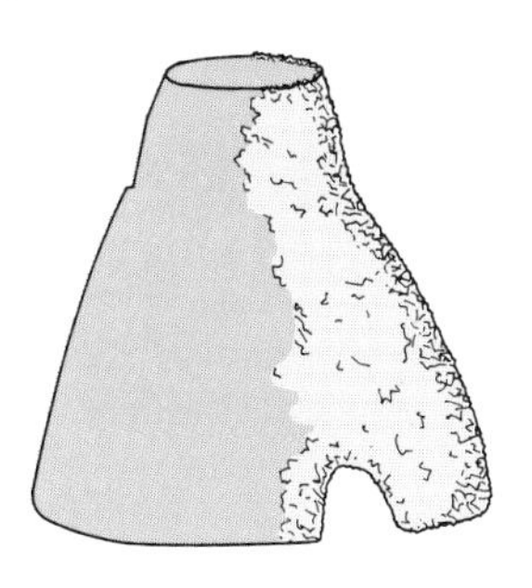

3. Spread a little glue on one part of the body and press plenty of fluff on. Cover the body a little at a time.

4. The head is two balls of wool, one half the size of the other. Sew the balls together and cover them with wool fluff, like the body.

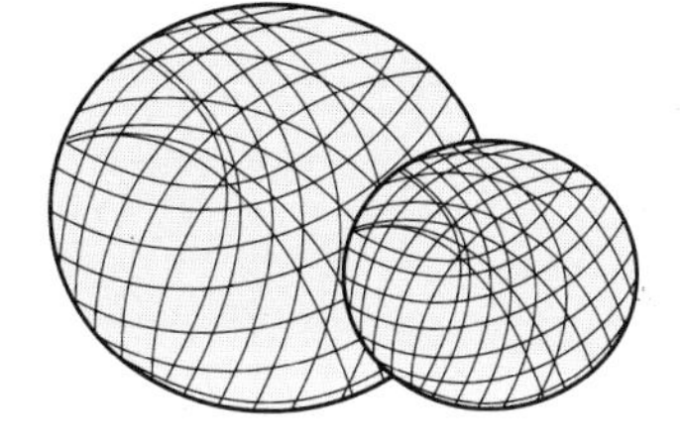

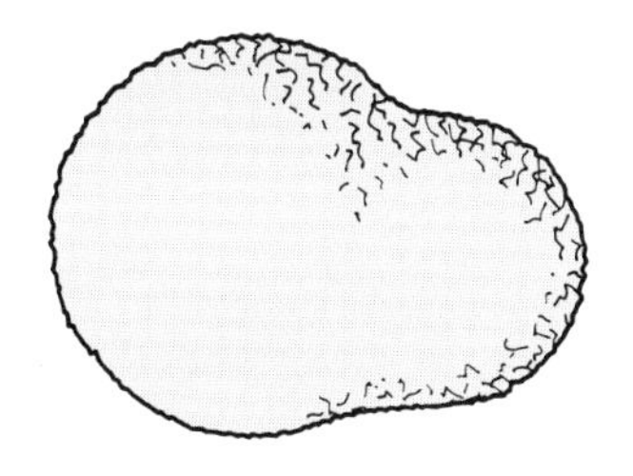

5. Cut out two pear-shaped felt pieces for the ears. A glued pleat gives them shape. Cover one side in fluff, then glue on to the head, facing forwards.

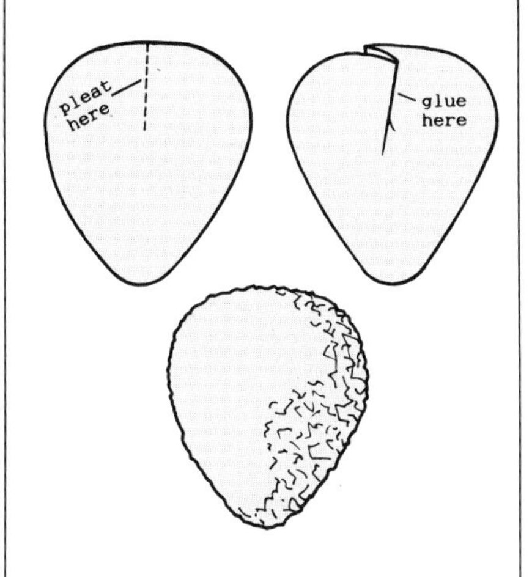

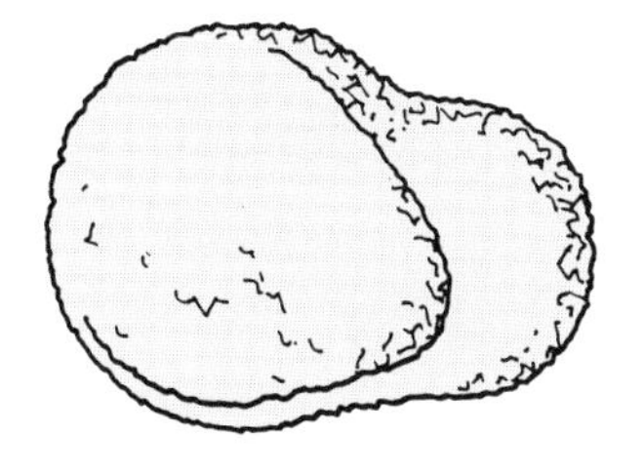

6. Use the point of closed scissors to make a hole for the nose. Glue in the button. Make two more holes and glue in the beads for the eyes. The tongue is a tiny scrap of pink felt. The tail is wool wound around a thin roll of paper. Make it thicker at one end and cover in wool fluff. Use a black felt pen to draw on the claws on the front paws.

7. Glue round the neck part of the body and stick the head on. Cover the join with more wool fluff.

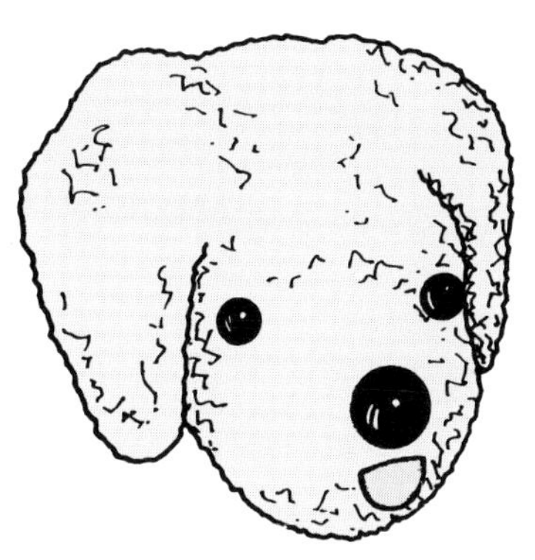

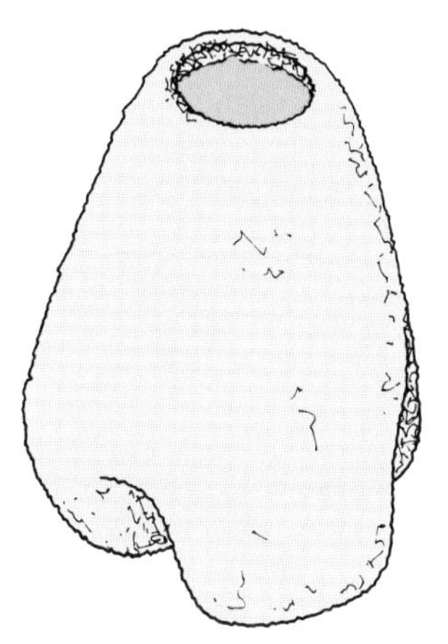

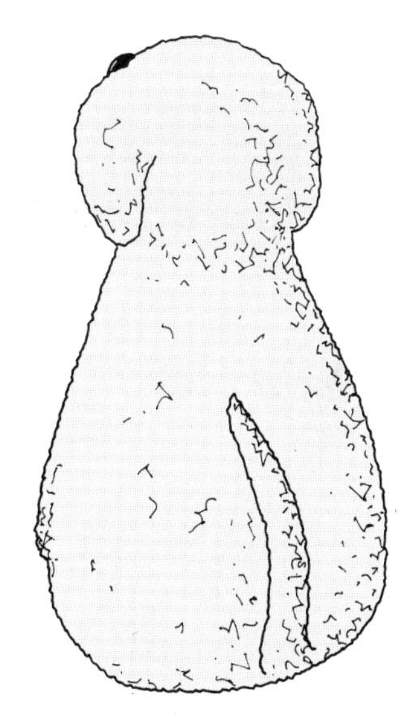

That's it! A little basket will be a nice home for the pups – especially if you make more than one.

Remember – these pups are models, not toys. The beads and button make them unsuitable for very young children to play with.

Blue Peter visits the Caribbean Islands

Sun-kissed beaches, golden sunsets, azure seas and breeze in the palm trees. Tropical sights and sounds.

Yes, there's plenty of that in the islands of the Caribbean. But as we discovered in our summer expedition to the West Indies, the tourist paradise is only part of the story.

The Caribbean has a giant arc of hundreds of islands stretching from the tip of Florida in the United States round to Venezuela at the top of South America. Its islands are rich and varied though not rich in terms of money. The first

things you notice are the hundreds of different trees all laden with fruit. Ripe mangoes, avocados, grapefruits, oranges and bananas all hang temptingly. The sea teems with fish; no one starves in the Caribbean.

But the islands have had a complicated and sad history – a history of invasion, slavery and cruelty. Most of the islands have their independence now from European colonial powers who ruled them for centuries – but not all.

We began our travels in the eastern Caribbean in a chain of islands called the Windwards. St Lucia was our first port of call – green and tropical, home of the world's only drive-in volcano (Soufrière) and lots of fun. Yvette had a quick introduction to how to dance Caribbean style at a street party on the first day! "She sure knows how to move," was the verdict from the locals . . .

A twenty-minute hop on a tiny plane that felt like it was held together with rubber bands, and we were in chic Martinique – altogether different from its neighbours. It's very French – not surprisingly as it *is* part of France. You speak French, drive French cars and eat lots of French bread! It's also the birthplace of one of France's most famous women: Josephine, wife of Napoleon Bonaparte. None of us had ever seen such a collection of beautiful yachts – but that was all part of Martinique's jet-set appeal, if you like that sort of thing.

The next stop was an island treasure – and without a doubt Diane's favourite – Dominica! A green and lush jewel containing the world's largest oceanic rainforest – a magical world of tiny plants and enormous trees, crystal clear forest pools and waterfalls waiting to be dived into. Far away from the tourist trail, here we visited one of the last remaining settlements of the Caribs – the Indian people who were the original inhabitants of the islands before the Europeans invaded.

The tiny island of Montserrat was recovering from the effects of the savage Hurricane Hugo that devastated the island only months before. Often called the Emerald Isle because of its similarity to Ireland, it seemed an odd setting for so many O'Reillys and shamrock emblems! It's also one of Britain's few remaining colonies. The Governor who runs the island is a direct representative of the Queen. The red post-office vans and telephone boxes certainly had a familiar look about them.

Our final destination was Jamaica: a big bustling island with one of the largest populations in the Caribbean. Blisteringly hot and noisy, it was a big shock after the quieter islands we had come from. Jamaica: home of reggae, rum and pirates!

◁ **John and Yvette as Captain Morgan and Annie Bonny, two of the fiercest pirates the Caribbean ever knew.**

▷ **Diane living it up.**

A POTTED HISTORY OF THE WEST INDIES

Christopher Columbus discovered the islands of the Caribbean five hundred years ago. That was the beginning of centuries of colonialism. Spain, Britain, France and Holland fought the fiercest sea battles in history over the islands – mostly over a very valuable commodity: not gold but sugar.

SUGAR SLAVERY

The islands are the perfect place to grow sugar – the climate is just right. When European adventurers first conquered lands here, they came to make money. More and more sugar was wanted back in Europe, so little by little the world's biggest sugar industry was created. Growing sugar is extremely tough and needs lots of labourers. Europeans weren't prepared to come and work – the problem had to be solved.

The solution lay in Africa. Slaves were brought in to work on the sugar plantations and the trade grew and grew. It went on for a long time – 350 years. That's three and a half centuries of people being stolen away from their families and bought and sold as objects. Nowadays the majority of people in the Caribbean are descended from African slaves.

The Caribbean was home to many vicious pirates. They plundered ships of their valuable cargoes and showed no mercy to anyone they captured. The British government turned a blind eye to piracy because many of their victims were Spanish ships. Britain and Spain were arch enemies in the Caribbean.

REGGAE

One of the Caribbean's best known exports is its music. The driving hypnotic beats of reggae are with you wherever you go. It has its roots in Jamaican folk music, which grew from the dance rhythms and sounds of African music. The most famous reggae superstar of all time, Bob Marley, lived in Kingston and sang about changing society and going back to African roots.

Birdie!

They run school trips with a difference at the Lee Valley Countryside Centre. Visitors travel from the Soviet Union fifteen hundred kilometres to Britain! And they fly all the way, dressed as birds! And they do it without even leaving London!

It all happens at the enormous Walthamstow Reservoirs, a great place to go bird-spotting. Thousands of migrating waterfowl head for it each spring. The Countryside Centre decided to combine a bit of bird-watching with an outdoor lesson on the environment. They get people to pretend they're migrating teal ducks, faced with the hazards of their long journey across Europe. Got your wings warmed up? Ready? Let's take off!

2

STOPPING POINT — RIVER ELBE

Next stop, the River Elbe in Germany. There's a nice friendly-looking forest; let's land. Suddenly, out of the trees – it's a FOX. Gobble, gulp, that's a teal making a tasty supper for a hungry fox. One more out of the game. Luckily, there are plenty left to fly on.

3

STOPPING POINT — IJSSELMEER

Over half-way now and time to call in at one of the flock's favourite watering-holes – Ijsselmeer in the Netherlands. The water seems so cool and inviting. But all black? It's OIL – oh, no – two more of the flock are lost, their feathers smothered by the sticky oil. The rest had better get out of here.

STOPPING POINT — WALTHAMSTOW

Almost home. Last stop is the Walthamstow Reservoirs. How glad the teal will be to see them. It's been a long, tough migration, what with the new buildings, predators and oil spillages to contend with. And for one member of the flock, the oldest, who's made this flight several times before, it's all too much. As the birds land in London, the old teal dies of exhaustion.

1

STOPPING POINT **LAKE LADOGA**

The birds like a nice rest once they get to Lake Ladoga. But what's this? A brand new factory built on their feeding ground! There's not enough food for all the birds – sadly, one or two die. That means they drop out of the game. For the rest, it's time to go again.

What an eventful journey! Some of the birds died, either from natural causes or from man's intervention. But most survived. They'll enjoy the summer, feed a great deal, then set off on the arduous migration back to their winter homeland in the Soviet Union.

△ **Watch the birdie! Adventure game over, Yvette tried to spot the real thing.**

The Greening of Blue Peter

UNLEADED

BLUE PETER's done dozens of "green" items and many viewers ask us "how green are you on the programme?" In this behind-the-scenes glimpse of the Blue Peter office, you'll find the answer is quite a dark shade of green!

Paper

THE Blue Peter office is always awash with paper. We read all the national newspapers and many regional ones. We receive masses of mail each day – most of the letters are from viewers and all those are kept. But many others aren't needed – things like press releases and invitations. They get recycled in a special "white paper" bin that all the programmes in our building use. We also recycle all our newspapers, and Daniel the recycling man comes along once a fortnight to take them away.

Recently, Blue Peter became the first programme in the BBC to use a special type of writing paper. It is not recycled paper, but paper from managed, renewable tree stocks. The main thing about it is that no chlorine is used to make the paper white. We've encouraged other programmes to use the same kind of paper and several have done so.

Inside the BBC, envelopes are reused many times, often until they're falling apart! For sending out letters, we use brown envelopes made of recycled paper. If you win a Blue Peter badge, it will arrive in one of our recycled-paper envelopes, and the letter that comes with it will be on our environmentally-friendly writing paper.

We cut the waste-paper mountain down to size by recycling paper.

Bottles & cans

Having run the largest-ever collection of aluminium cans with the BabyLife Appeal, we try to save all the bottles and cans we use for recycling. Lots of people like to buy bottled drinks from the BBC snack bar, so we end up with quite a few by the end of the week. Sally, our production secretary, loves Diet Coke and ends up with a mountain of cans on her desk – she made a pretty big contribution to the BabyLife Appeal on her own!

Getting to work

This is one area where the report is "could do better". We did a survey of everyone in the Blue Peter office. Here are the results:

Drive in by car	45%
Use public transport	31%
Walk	17%
Ride a bike	7%

Most of the car drivers travel alone, which is very unfriendly to the environment. Many more could be walking or using public transport, so perhaps there'll be some improvement in 1992! One bright spot – 92% of all the car drivers surveyed use unleaded petrol – that's well above the national average.

Make-up

Most people you see on television – men as well as women – are wearing make-up. That's because the bright lights would make their skin shine if they had no powder on their faces. When Diane looked into the subject, she discovered that the make-up used in the BBC contains ingredients that have been tested on animals. Yvette and John quickly agreed with her idea that all the make-up used on Blue Peter must be cruelty-free. We are the first BBC programme to have this policy and hope that other programmes will follow our lead.

DIY Hairstyles

Things were getting pretty hairy in the Blue Peter studio when a group of young trends were making waves with some zany new hair-dos. They were enjoying the fringe benefits of do-it-yourself hairdressing and looking a cut above at the same time!

Crimpers, gels, tongs, mousses, hairdriers and straighteners were at the ready as wild styles were created in a matter of minutes. Our team of young stylists was experimenting with new looks that could be created easily for a party or night out.

So if you're worried about friends crimping your style, look no further!

△ **Claire's spiky look is created by taking 3-cm-wide sections of hair all the way round the hairline and dividing each section lengthwise into ten equal parts. Wind seam-binding or ribbon tightly round the bottom of each bunch so that you have a section of bound hair that stands up on its own, with a little sprouting ponytail on the top.**

Wired Plait Mohican

◁ **Chloe's straight locks were transformed into a wild Mohican look. The stand-up effect is achieved with pipe-cleaners – no need for any gel or spray!**

STAGE 1

Divide hair into six sections across your head and tie into ponytails.

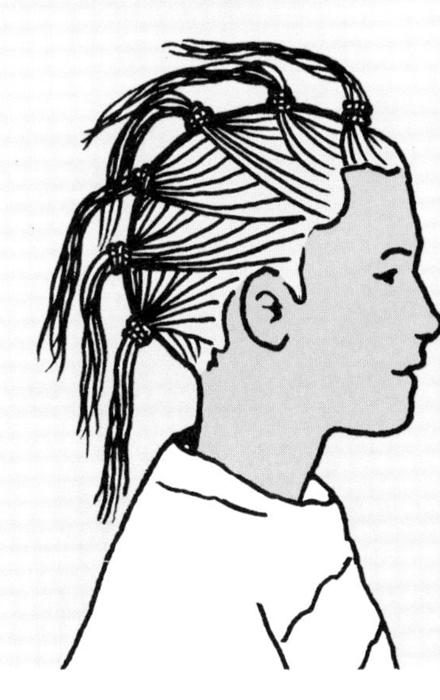

△ Tyrone's close shaved "M. C. Hammer look" was spruced up with pomade to give a glossy shine for real street cred.

Have a go yourself and see if you can come up with any more wacky hair-raising ideas, like John's "Tin-Tin look"!

STAGE 2

Plait each ponytail holding a pipe-cleaner with one of the hair strands. Each plait uses one pipe-cleaner.

STAGE 3

Wrap another pipe-cleaner round the base of a plait and bend it backwards so it curves round and touches the base of the plait behind.

STAGE 4

Bend the next plait round in the same way until you reach the last. Leave plait at back hanging. Hey presto!

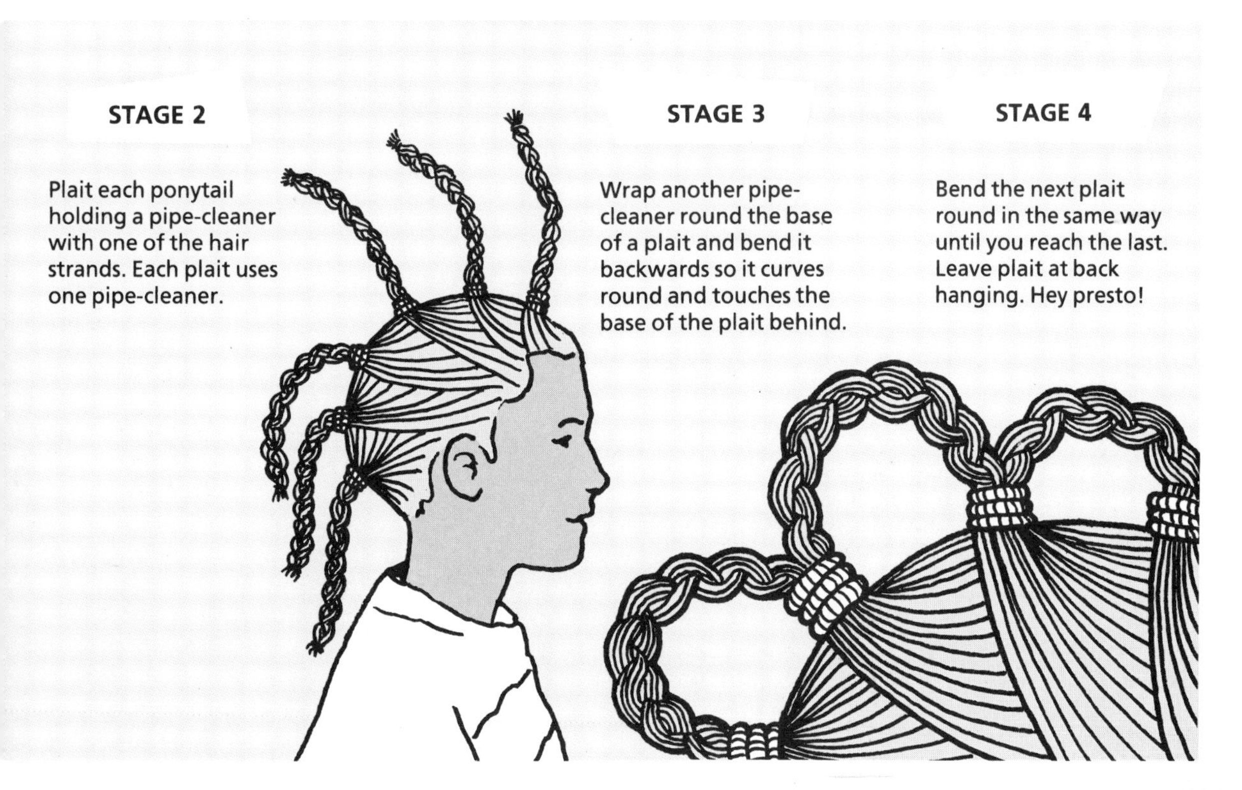

A REAL CLIFFHANGER

Blue Peter presenters are lucky enough to try anything – especially things they don't want to do!

Yvette had never been climbing when it was suggested she might try. Game for anything, she agreed immediately, but was probably having second thoughts when she was dangling at the end of a rope, clutching a smooth cliff face, with boiling sea lashing the rocks sixty metres below!

For her first taste of rock climbing, Yvette was taken by ex-Royal Marine John Barry to Bosigran Cliffs in Cornwall.

Properly kitted out with tough climbing helmets, sticky-soled climbing boots and a rope, they were off, John disappearing quickly into the crevices of the cliff.

"Come on Yvette, just let your legs and feet do the work, don't hang from your arms."

Yvette had trouble making her first step, trying to find somewhere to put her feet on the smooth rock, but soon she was off. "Take small steps," she told herself, remembering the advice John had given her.

◀ **Yvette with her climbing instructor, John Barry.**

▼ **Cliff climbing, step one: trim fingernails. Long nails make for tricky gripping.**

▽ **"Climbing's so much fun – let's do it again!"**

"Whatever you do, don't let go!"

△ **"We can't go on meeting like this!" Yvette and John celebrate reaching the summit.**

◁ **A tricky bit – Yvette ponders her next move.**

It was tiring and tough, but when Yvette paused to look down, she was surprised at how high she was. Luckily, she's not afraid of heights. Then came the really awkward bit, about half-way up. Yvette had to swing to her right across a jutting out boulder.

"I'm going to fall, I'm going to fall!"

"No, you're not," came the voice from above. John had the rope connecting them, so even if Yvette *did* fall, it would only be a couple of metres before he hauled her up.

"Come on, lady, come *on*," muttered Yvette to herself, and with a heave she was over the difficult bit.

It wasn't long before she reached the summit and was able to look around at the wonderful Cornish view from sixty metres up.

"For one awful moment, I did think I was going to fall," said Yvette, "but I really did enjoy that!"

◁ **"How high am I now?" Still a long way to go, Yvette!**

DARCEY PROFILE BUSSELL

The day Darcey Bussell came to the Blue Peter studio was a day like no other.

For once the whole studio was silent. Floor managers, cameramen, presenters, even Willow gazed on, transfixed by her grace and poise. She was dancing the lead role in *The Prince of the Pagodas* – a part created for her by world-famous choreographer Sir Kenneth Macmillan.

Darcey's story is every young dancer's dream. At the age of twenty-one she is the Royal Ballet's newest star. She rocketed to fame to become their youngest principal dancer. She's been called the "dancer of the decade",

"the new Margot Fonteyn", "the new princess".

Her career began as a schoolgirl ballet dancer. "We used to go to dance class every Saturday," she told John. "I enjoyed it more than my friends." She decided to try for the Royal Ballet School at the age of thirteen. There was no stopping her then. Blue Peter spotted her five years ago when she was a young hopeful and three years after that she was noticed by Kenneth Macmillan and launched on the path to stardom!

Darcey's long legs, easy confidence and distinctive style will see that she steals the spotlight for years to come.

Snow in the Summertime

Do you remember June 1991? One of the memorable things about it was the awful weather that bega the month – snow in Scotland, frost in the Midlands, cold and rainy everywhere.

All the same, Yvette was a bit surprised when she was told she was off to do some winter sports. There was no flight to Austria or Switzerland in store but a short drive down the M4 motorway to Bracknell in Berkshire.

That's where the John Nike Sports Complex is geared up for a kinds of winter sports, whatever the weather. Dry ski slopes are nothing new, but Yvette was there to try . . . tobogganing!

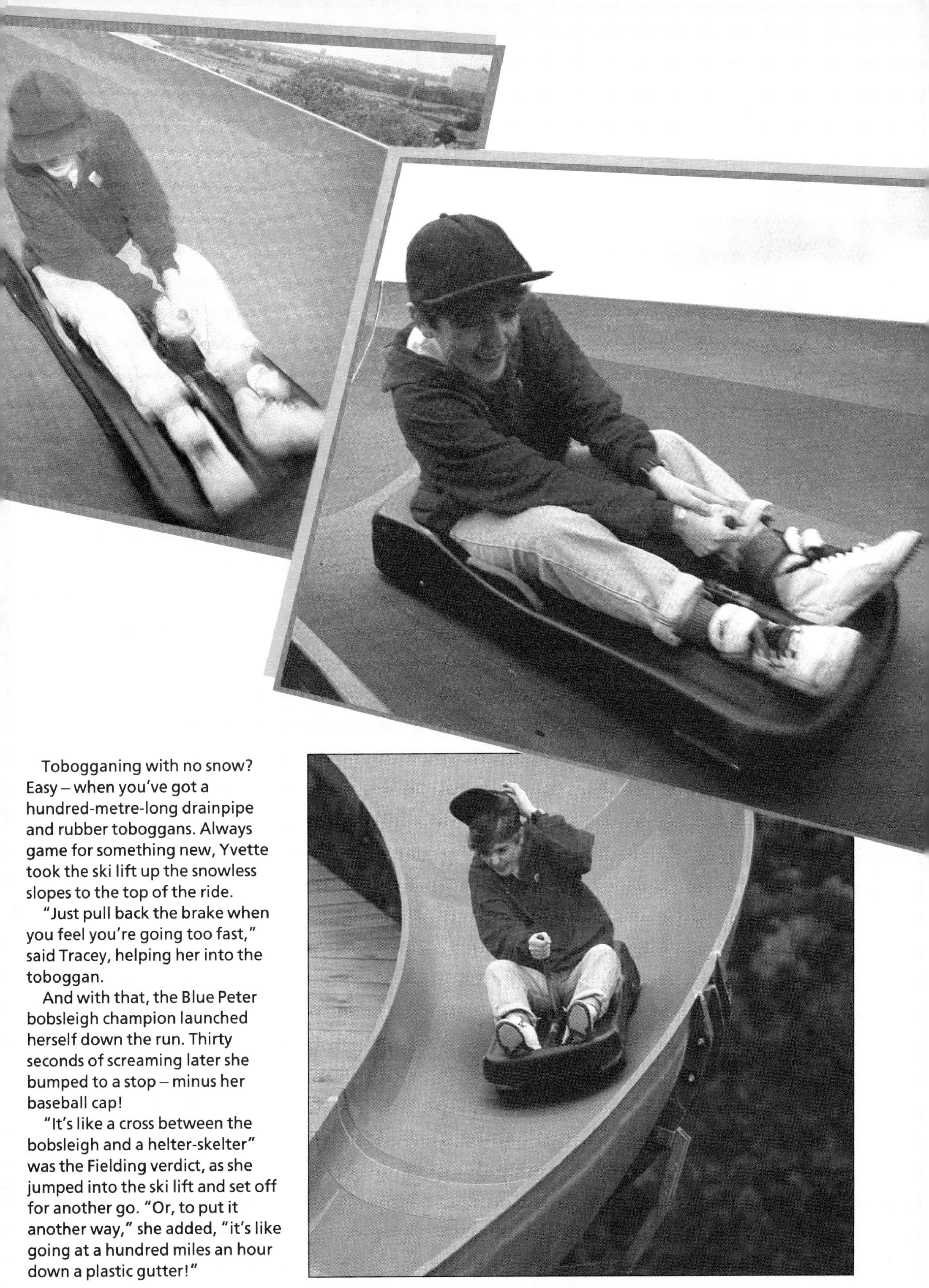

Tobogganing with no snow? Easy – when you've got a hundred-metre-long drainpipe and rubber toboggans. Always game for something new, Yvette took the ski lift up the snowless slopes to the top of the ride.

"Just pull back the brake when you feel you're going too fast," said Tracey, helping her into the toboggan.

And with that, the Blue Peter bobsleigh champion launched herself down the run. Thirty seconds of screaming later she bumped to a stop – minus her baseball cap!

"It's like a cross between the bobsleigh and a helter-skelter" was the Fielding verdict, as she jumped into the ski lift and set off for another go. "Or, to put it another way," she added, "it's like going at a hundred miles an hour down a plastic gutter!"

Wolfgang Amadeus Mozart

There can't be many people who have never heard the name Mozart or who wouldn't recognize at least *one* Mozart tune. Lots of familiar and famous melodies are Mozart's – the Horse of the Year Show theme to name but one!

This year is an important one for music lovers because it is two hundred years since the composer died. During his short life he created a vast quantity of music: songs, concertos, operas, symphonies. In fact he created two hundred hours of music – music that's understood all over the world and sums up every human feeling.

John enjoying an Austrian coffee overlooking Salzburg, the beautiful city where Mozart was born.

His trail-blazing career began when he was only four years old. As a child superstar, he was taken all over Europe by his ambitious father to dazzle the rich and famous with his outstanding talent. The Mozarts travelled to Germany, France, Holland, Belgium and England – all in a drafty old carriage. It wasn't a normal childhood, but then Mozart wasn't a normal child. He was to spend a third of his life travelling.

As he grew up, his music became more and more extraordinary. He took Italy by storm with his first opera, but when he returned to his home town of Salzburg, in Austria, he didn't fit in and opted to move to Vienna, where the music scene was livelier. He was a huge success. He gave concerts, took on pupils and was given commissions to compose. He lived well and spent well, went to the best parties and loved to fool around. He was also one of the best billiards players in Europe.

In some ways Mozart was ahead of his time and not everyone could keep up with him. His earlier successes didn't last in Vienna. When he died of a fever at the age of just thirty-five, he was penniless. Today he is remembered as one of the greatest musical geniuses the world has ever known – if not *the* greatest.

The magnificent Vienna State Opera where Mozart's works are often performed.

THE STORY OF MOZART'S LIFE

Aged three, he climbed on to the piano stool and played his sister's pieces perfectly. He was composing songs at five and symphonies at eight.

His father, keen to show off the wonder-child, took him to the Schönbrunn Palace to play before Empress Maria Theresa. He dazzled everyone with musical tricks.

Arriving in Vienna, he soon won the hearts of the upper classes and became the toast of the town.

His music was so new and exciting it wasn't appreciated by everyone. The Emperor said his new opera had "too many notes". Mozart cheekily replied, "Just as many as necessary".

Mozart liked the good life and spent his money easily. He got into debt and died poor and exhausted.

DINOSAURS ALIVE

There were more than one or two worried, not to say downright nervous, faces the day the dinosaurs came to the Blue Peter studio!

OK, so you might know dinosaurs died out sixty-five million years ago. But when an eleven-metre-long Allosaurus bares its fangs at you, you have a lot of difficulty believing it's just a model.

We've had dinosaurs in the studio before, but nothing quite like Allosaurus and its smaller, but equally vicious, cousin Deinonychus. They were life-size and complete in every detail, with scaly skin and enormous teeth. They were brought to life by animatronics, in the same way film-makers make models move. Allosaurus could roar, raise and lower its head, roll its eyes, open and shut its mouth – all at once!

Any reconstruction by model-makers has to rely largely on guesswork – nobody knows for sure what colours Allosaurus and Deinonychus were – but these guesses were so convincing that you could imagine yourself coming face to face with the toothsome twosome in a prehistoric swamp, instead of confronting a load of plastic and compressed air pipes in a television studio.

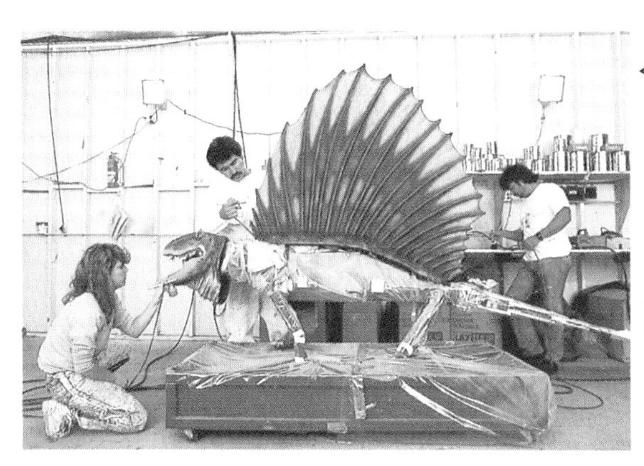

◁ **A Dimetrodon gets a coat of spray paint.**

▷ **The robotic working of an Apatosaurus is tested.**

And these two were real brawlers in the dinosaur world. Both were meat eaters – Allosaurus had over seventy teeth and massive jaws to clamp shut on its prey. Deinonychus was smaller – about the size of a wolf – but just as vicious. Hunting in packs, it could take on dinosaurs twice its size.

Dinosaurs ruled the earth millions of years ago and died out long before humans evolved. They have left only their fossilized remains as clues for the animatronic experts to produce life-size robotic dinosaurs. But as anyone who has gazed in wonder at a Tyrannosaurus or Triceratops skeleton will know, the fascination of the dinosaurs lives on. For one day on Blue Peter, we all felt as if we were alongside them – and it was not a pretty sight!

◁ What came first, the dinosaur or the egg? A Parasaurolophus hatches in its animatronic nest.

▽ Deinonychus was a small, meat-eating dinosaur. It ran fast on its hind legs and used its big eyes to look for prey, which it held with its sharp front claws. People used to think all dinosaurs were slow and lumbering, but fossils like Deinonychus made them believe that some were fast and intelligent, with large brains.

Smoky Fish Supreme

Cook up a fishy surprise with John's tasty idea for tea! Fish is cheap, healthy, and it doesn't have to come in fingers or wrapped in newspaper! Smoky Fish Supreme is easy to make, and it'll stuff four hungry tums in less time than it takes to say "Shiver me timbers"!

Here's what you need

500 g smoked haddock fillets (skinned)
250 g long grain rice
1 vegetable stock cube, dissolved in a litre of boiling water
250 g frozen peas
4 tablespoons of milk
225 g grated cheese – Cheddar is fine
a little butter, salt and pepper

Here's how you make it

There are three lots of cooking in this recipe. You cook the rice in one pan and the fish in another. Then you put it all together and cook it a bit more. Here's what you do:

Dissolve the stock cube in the boiling water. BE CAREFUL – get someone to help. Add the rice, and cook it for about fifteen minutes. Add the frozen peas, and cook for five more minutes.

Meanwhile (proper cooking, this) put the fish in a largish frying pan, with the butter and milk. Cook it on a gentle heat for about eight to twelve minutes, depending on how thick the fish is. By the way, you don't have to use haddock. Plaice or cod fillets will be fine. Smoked fish will be tastiest.

When the fish is cooked, use a spatula to put it in an oven-proof dish *that is big enough to take the rice and peas too*. Delicately break the fish into flakes with a fork. Stir in the rice and peas. Add some salt and pepper and half the grated cheese. Mix it all up and smooth it down with the fork.

Almost finished! Tell everyone tea's ready. Pile on the rest of the cheese and stick the whole thing under a hot grill for a couple of minutes. Serve it as soon as the cheese is melted and golden brown. Enjoy!

Blue Peter Presenter

Yvette Fielding

"There's one experience that will stay with me forever," says Yvette, looking back over a packed series of Blue Peter shows.

"My three visits to Romania are unforgettable. Being able to play with the children in the orphanages I visited, and being able to give some love and time to children who hadn't had any, was something I'd not experienced before."

Back home, Yvette's rally-driving film is something she remembers fondly. "I loved it, especially almost beating John over a timed course."

Another happy memory is her visit to the White Cliffs Experience in Dover. "Two days in a museum – and I wasn't bored once!"

Even Blue Peter takes second place to the biggest event in Yvette's life during 1991 – getting engaged and married. Good luck to Yvette and Barry!

How many of Yvette's souvenirs pictured on this page can you match to Blue Peter events? Answers on page 61.

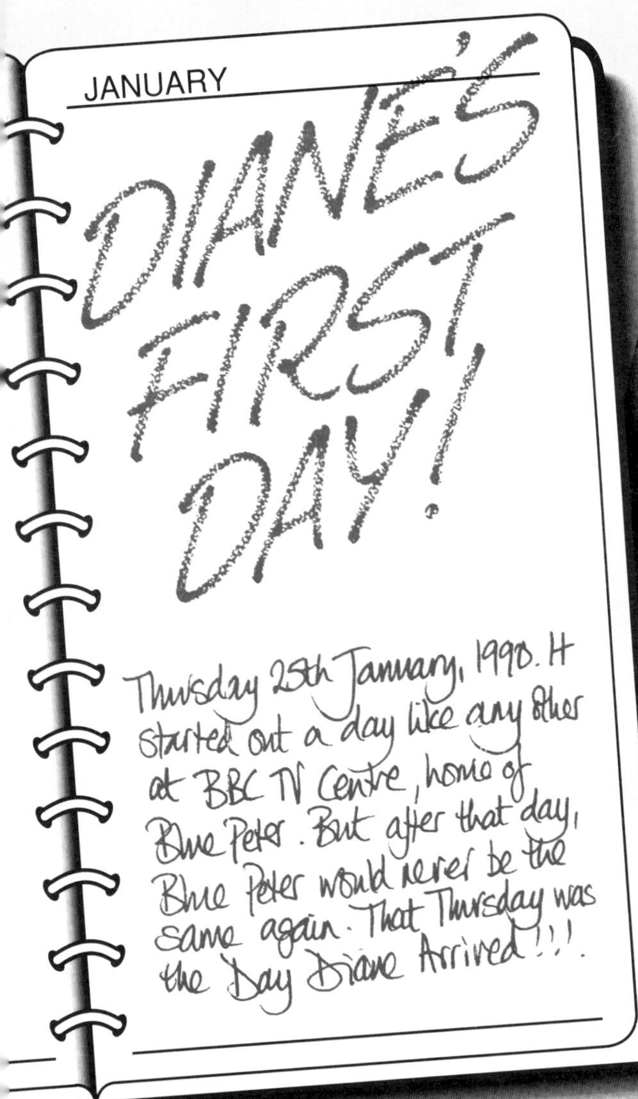

am

8.30 A very battered, dirty grey-green 1955 Morris Minor arrives at the main entrance. The commissionaire tries to tell the driver that the scrap metal dealer is on the other side of the road. The driver insists that she is the new Blue Peter presenter, and the lump of metal she's inside is her favourite thing in the world.

(Diane's Morris Minor had a brief but glorious life on Blue Peter. It starred in its own film – the London to Brighton Morris Minor Run – but then died when it was clobbered by another car. Luckily, it's strongly built, and protected Diane from injury. It awaits repairs . . .)

9.00 First job – buy cups of tea for Yvette and John (are they trying to tell her something?).

9.15 If starting on Blue Peter isn't enough for one day, the production team have decided that a film crew will follow Diane around, making a film to show on the next Blue Peter, entitled "Diane's First Day". At this rate, her first day could be her last!

10.00 Diane arrives in the studio for rehearsals. She's no stranger to television, having presented Corners, but she's surprised by the speed at which everything has to be done to get Blue Peter ready for the live transmission at 5.05.

pm

1.00 Lunchtime in the BBC canteen with Yvette and John. They tell Diane that the first day is nothing compared to what comes afterwards! They all agree that nerves are the biggest problem at first.

2.00 Back in the studio, and help from Yvette deciding which outfit to wear. The green mini-dress gets the nod!

3.45 The programme run-through – Diane's last chance to rehearse. She only has a little bit to do about antique rocking horses but she wants to get it exactly right.

4.55 Ten minutes to go. A huge bunch of flowers arrives – it's a good luck gift from the whole team. At the last minute, Diane pins on her new Blue Peter badge and walks out to the studio floor.

5.05 The famous theme tune plays and the programme's on the air. Seven and a half million people watch as Diane is introduced by Yvette and John. "Let's meet her, Blue Peter's eighteenth presenter, Diane-Louise Jordan!"

5.35 Twenty-five minutes have rushed by. Diane was nervous, but it all went very well. Yvette and John rush up to congratulate her – the most difficult moment for a new presenter is over. Diane-Louise Jordan has arrived!

THE CHANNEL

DOVER

For centuries people have stood on the White Cliffs of Dover gazing over the twenty-mile divide between Britain and continental Europe.

Some were inspired to devise clever schemes to join the two countries, and construction even began on a couple of occasions but came to nothing. That is, until December 1990, when tunnellers from France and Britain met under the middle of the English Channel. The central service tunnel was complete, joining Britain and Europe for the first time in twelve thousand years.

When the Channel Tunnel opens in 1993, the hovercraft and ferries will no longer be the only option when crossing to France. Huge shuttle trains will carry cars, lorries and their passengers to France in around thirty-five minutes. International express trains will run direct from Paris to London in three hours.

THE GRAPHIC

AN ILLUSTRATED WEEKLY NEWSPAPER

SATURDAY, MARCH 4, 1882

FRONT ELEVATION

REAR ELEVATION

SIDE ELEVATION

TUNNEL

SANGATTE

Tunnelling on the French side had its problems. The tunnel route passed through wetter rock, making digging more difficult. The solution was to sink an enormous waterproof shaft, sixty-five metres deep and fifty-six metres wide, to start the tunnelling in better conditions.

What to do with the millions of tons of rock that come out could cause a huge environmental problem. But it's been carefully thought out. On the French side the rock or "spoil" is mixed with water and pumped to a huge man-made lake. In time the water will drain away, leaving a landscaped hill. The British spoil is brought out as rock and dumped behind a new sea wall, forming an area of reclaimed land at the bottom of Shakespeare Cliff.

John travelled out along a stretch of new under-sea tunnel in a "manrider" used to ferry workers to the face. "It was dark, damp, incredibly noisy but full of atmosphere. It was amazingly exciting seeing for real one of the greatest engineering projects the world has ever known."

▽ Giant moles called TBMs dig the tunnels. They grind away at the rock at up to four hundred metres every week. Guided by lasers, they are like mini-factories. They leave a completed concrete-lined tunnel behind them and even have a rest room where the workers can get a cup of coffee, one hundred metres below the sea bed!

Three tunnels are being constructed – two to carry the trains in both directions and a smaller one in the centre, the service tunnel. It's for emergencies and maintenance.

Every 375 metres is a cross-passageway which joins the running tunnels with the service tunnel. On each side eight kilometres out to sea are giant cross-over points where the trains can be routed on to the other track. They are known as *cathedrals* – the largest under-sea spaces in the world.

Blue Peter Presenter

John Leslie

For a chap who's run his first marathon, trained with the London Monarchs, and is generally a bit of an all-round athlete, John picks a surprising highlight for his Blue Peter year.

"Mozart, without a doubt," says John. "Although it was minus ten (and I hate the cold), Salzburg and Vienna were beautiful and the people delightful. While we were waiting to film at the Schönbrunn Palace in Vienna, I was listening to a Mozart tape on my cassette player. It all seemed to come together – the scenery, the palace, the music – all exactly right."

Music also provided John's other big moment of the series – when he conducted an orchestra at the Schools' Prom at the Royal Albert Hall. "Probably the toughest thing I did all year. Going out on that stage was nerve-racking – even worse than my first day on Blue Peter. But the euphoria during the last bars of Bizet's *Carmen* matched saving a penalty from Denis Law!"

How many of John's souvenirs pictured on this page can you match to Blue Peter events? Answers on page 61.

A very big Speug!

> “Twa wee burdies, sat on a barra,
> One was a Speug
> And the other a sparra!”

What on earth is a Speug?

You might know if you live in Glasgow. It's a "cheeky wee brown bird", as John described the very large Speug that landed in the Blue Peter studio.

Our Speug was cheeky, but by no means wee! It was six metres long, three metres high, and unlike any sparra. It was designed by a famous Scottish sculptor, George Wyllie, for the 1991 Arts is Magic Festival, held in Glasgow.

Mr Wyllie made the head and body of the massive Speug out of metal – but he did not bother making any feathers. Instead, he asked children from all over Scotland to make the feathers out of pieces of paper. Every feather had a question on it, such as "When will Glasgow Rangers win the Cup?" or "When will people stop polluting the River Clyde?"

It was a lot of fun to read the feathers when the Speug flew into the studio, but there was a more serious idea behind the questions. The organisers of the Arts is Magic Festival plan to put all the questions on a computer and have an up-to-date record of what children in 1991 want to know.

So the Speug now has thousands of questions stuck to it. If it knows the answers, it's not saying – not even a cheep!

NIGHTMARE IN NORWAY!

Only madmen and Blue Peter presenters would consider jumping into an ice hole filled with arctic-cold water in the middle of a particularly harsh Scandinavian winter! But as Diane found, that's all part of the job. The challenge set, she joined the Arctic and Mountain Warfare Cadre on a routine training exercise high in the snow-covered mountains of Norway.

The Norwegian winter is so cold that the Royal Marines use it to learn how to survive in the cruellest of weather conditions. They are taught to cope with temperatures of forty degrees below freezing.

Colour Sergeant Dave Stocks is a Mountain Leader and was Diane's guide as she ventured higher and higher into the mountains in a snow-cat.

"I'll look after you and you look after me," he advised. In temperatures so low that you've got to be careful to avoid frostbite, and with areas you can't see yourself, like face and ears, you

have to rely on someone else's eagle eye.

It wasn't long before Diane's moment arrived. She looked on in horror as the Marine in front of her plunged headlong into the icy cold waters. It was all about learning to survive a potentially lethal fall through the ice.

As she stood waiting for her turn, she couldn't believe there was a good purpose for this exercise. But Dave's instructions were clear: "As soon as you hit the water," he said, attaching the safety rope and skis, "drag yourself out kicking with your feet. Some Swedes do it regularly after taking a sauna!" he reassured, unsuccessfully.

Splash!! Before she knew it, she was up to her neck in paralysing freezing water. Scrambling madly to escape the bitter cold, she bawled, "I can't believe it, this is the coldest I've ever been in my life. I'm so proud of myself!" After a rapid roll in the snow to dry off, she jumped into the Land Rover to recover. An experience not to be repeated!

VILLAGE CAMERA

Have you ever wanted to know about the history of your town or village? Have you ever wondered what your Granny was like when she was young, or even what life was like a century ago?

The children of Sapperton village school set about finding out the answers to questions like these when a little bit of their local history went up in smoke.

When an old man from the village died, he left behind a treasure trove of old photos and mementos from the past. Unfortunately, his house was cleared and lots of old "junk" was thrown on to a bonfire – lost forever. Determined that it should never happen again, the children were spurred into action to discover their village history – before more of it disappeared.

Talking to old villagers, grandparents and great aunts, the Sapperton children uncovered a wealth of photos and local tales that drew a vivid picture of life a hundred years ago. The kind of people who hoard things long after they seem to be useful proved to be a wonderful source of information. Old boxes of greying snaps and scrapbooks hidden in attics were brimming with history.

With the help of school headmistress Miss Pinnell, the information was turned into *Village Camera*, a unique record of Gloucestershire village life.

Nora Annesley was born ninety years ago in

◁ *Sapperton schoolchildren experience life in the schoolroom of a hundred years ago.*

▽ *Dressing up in old clothes helps to bring history to life.*

Sapperton. She lives in Surrey now but told lots of stories. She described her school day at Sapperton: "Arithmetic was always the first lesson of the day, followed by English, History, Geography and Reading until 12 o'clock."

She also told the story of Mrs Carrington, a Liberal supporter (the Liberals were not popular in Sapperton), who boasted when her MP was elected. Late one night the Conservatives painted her door blue. The incident caused a real stir and was talked about for weeks afterwards. No one ever found out who did it.

Moira Gobey, the school cook, lived by the canal tunnel as a child. It was such a popular spot for walking that she and her mother used to provide afternoon teas. Her grandfather was responsible for the upkeep of the canal for many miles. Today the house and canal are in ruins.

Local historian Stan Gardiner told the sad story of Gerald Drummond, a young photographer who was killed in the war. His parents were so heartbroken that they locked up his room just as it was. It remained locked until the house was sold years later.

If you want to find out more about where you live or where your family come from, you could start by chatting to your Granny. You might be amazed at what stories are hidden in the old family album right under your nose.

Dear Blue Peter

My classmates and I found a little hedgehog crawling around in the grass outside our classroom which was being mowed at the time. Our teacher brought it in, and our head master got an empty fish tank to keep it in until the end of school, and then Caroline palmer is going to take it home to look after it until it is well enough to go free

yours sincerely

Katherine west age 10

Dear Blue Peter

me and my friend have fo
a hedgehog in my back ga
I have been feeding him
kitty kat he is eatting it very
from Gareth Jones

Dear Blue peter

2 Days ago.

I watched Blue peter. Today we found a hedgehog in garden at mid-morn

It weighed 400 gram so I knew that it was no well. how much Do the have to weigh to be able to hibernate?

love from Christopher Taylor age 6

Dear Blue Peter,

I was very intrested in yestedays programme especially the part about hedgehogs. My mum rescues hedgehog and I help her when I can. I took one into school my school (Greenhayes School for boys) to show everyone how nice hedgehogs are and not to hurt them with chemicals in the garden etc. We have five at the moment including two badly brai damaged ones called Daphne and Snowy, they will have to stay with us for the r of our lives. They live in a big border and the vegetable patch. We have rescued and released about twenty hedgehogs so far. I enclose a photograph of a fe of the orphans we had.

I enjoy your programme very much and watch it whenever I don't have too much homework.

Yours sincerely

Edward Ames

Dear

Blue Peter

The night after I watched your programme I found a hedgehog on my school field. I took it in to the classroom and weighed it. It weighed under 400grams so I took it home. We fed it on cat and dog food and kept it warm in the garage. That night my mum rang up a hedgehog care centre in Louth. The man said we would have to keep it through the winter and set it free in spring but we thought it was better to put it into care. Please tell everyone to go careful and look after hedgehogs and wildlife!

Yours faithfully

Marie O'Shea

xxxx

If we ever want a new pet for Blue Peter, we'll probably choose a hedgehog! They must be Blue Peter viewers' favourite little mammals!

Our hedgehog tales began with a report from the Wildlife Hospital, St Tiggywinkle's, in Aylesbury. Les Stocker, who's made something of a name for himself by caring for injured and abandoned hedgehogs, told Yvette that winter is a bad time for the prickly little beasties. "If you see one out and about, especially during the day, it's probably in trouble," warned Les.

His advice – take it in, keep it warm, and weigh it. Any hedgehog weighing less than 600 grams is too small to hibernate through the winter and needs caring for. The best thing to feed them with is cat or dog food. Hedgehogs are meat-eaters, but they are greedy, so they'll probably eat anything, even if it's no good for them. Les says bread and milk, which many people feed tame hedgehogs, is very bad for them – they can't digest milk properly and need the goodness they get from meat.

Les thinks people could be more careful around their gardens. Hedgehogs will crawl into old bottles and tins, and they can get trapped in strawberry netting – so keep the place tidy. Hedgehogs are useful to have around – they love to eat garden pests like beetles, slugs and snails – so it's worth making sure your garden is a safe place for them. One big danger spot is under bonfires. Fork the pile over to check nothing is underneath before you set light to the fire.

After Les was filmed, letters poured in. Some viewers asked for advice, while others told us about hedgehogs they had rescued. Some of their letters are on this page. Louisa Udall certainly knows all about hedgehog traps – she sent us the actual plastic drinks-can ring binder that almost killed the hedgie she rescued.

It turns out that Blue Peter viewers are keen to do their bit to help Britain's hedgehogs. If you want to find out more, you could get Les Stocker's book, *The Complete Hedgehog*, from your library. Or you could contact St Tiggywinkle's. You'll find the details at the back of this book.

Happy hedgehogging!!

▽ *Just a few of the prickly tales sent in by hedgehog-happy Blue Peter viewers! Louisa Udall (above left) rescued a hedgehog after it got its head stuck in a plastic ring binder used to hold drinks-cans.*

JOHN MEETS THE LONDON MONARCHS

What are all the numbers for?... *...Seems easy enough...* *...Uh oh, looks lik*

"Armstrong's my name, training's my game. What seems to be the problem, John?" the London Monarchs' trainer asked in a broad Louisiana drawl. "I've got a problem with my shoulder," John replied sheepishly. In moments he was being straightened out for a morning practice session with American Football's newest team.

Treatment successfully completed, Number 1's next appointment was in the locker room. Shoulder pads big enough to make a dent in any door frame, leg guards, crash helmet and face mask – all vital ingredients to provide protection.

Out on the field, for the first time in his life John Leslie was dwarfed. He actually felt small as the line of giants couldn't wait to take him on.

First, a gentle introduction to the sport by learning to throw and catch the ball – even this was harder than it looked! A lifetime of playing soccer is no preparation for coping with a "spinning torpedo".

Quarterback is a key position. The quarterback tries to steer clear of trouble. But this was where John found out what "taking a hit" really meant. A collision with 250 pounds of American steel was like being blown away.

"I couldn't believe the impact. It was like being hit by a juggernaut. And if that wasn't enough, I couldn't understand what everyone was shouting . . ."

By the end of the session, battered and bruised, John scored his first touchdown – enough to convince him that this sport was worth taking a look at. The following Sunday, the new recruit joined the crowd of 50,000 at Wembley, cheering on the London Monarchs as they took on the New York Knights. John was glad to witness their 22–18 victory – but from the safety of the terraces this time!

◁ **Number 1 joins the A Team!**

▷ **The Crown Jewels, the Monarchs' cheerleaders, preparing for the big match in the Blue Peter studio.**

Make

Edd the Duck

Olympic Superstar!

Edd's the British team's mascot for the Barcelona Olympics. Help him cheer on our team by making your own Edd glove puppet, dressed in an Olympic-style jogging suit. Awesome!

You will need

A yellow foam sponge ball
Yellow wool
Bright green wool (for his hair)
Kitchen-roll tube
Old white vest or T-shirt fabric
Orange and yellow felt
Glue

The head

1. Use the marking on the ball to make a downward sloping slit – that will be Edd's mouth. You can do it by snipping carefully along the line with scissors. Taking that as a guide, make another slit where his hair will go. Below the mouth, cut out a hole about the size of a 10p piece.

2. Wind the yellow wool around four fingers about 10 times. Carefully cut through the loops to make strands. Snip off pieces 0.5 cm long.

3. Spread a little glue at a time on the head and press plenty of fluff on. Cover the head.

4. Fold 10-cm bundles of the green wool in half. Glue them into the hair slit.

5. Stick the orange and yellow pieces of felt together. The pieces should be about the size of a large biscuit, with the yellow piece slightly larger. Fold the felt so the yellow is on the outside. Stick it into the mouth slit in the head.

6. Edd's eyes are small oval pieces of white paper. Use a black felt-tip to draw in the pupils. Draw them looking down.

The jogging suit

1. Cut an oblong of the white material, 14 cm × 24 cm, and fold it in half. Cut a small semi-circle out of the folded end – that's for the neck.

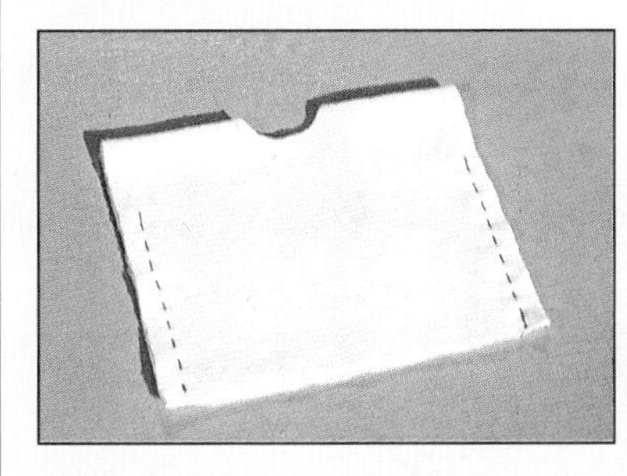

2. Sew or glue the sides up, leaving small holes at the top for Edd's hands.

3. Cut mitt shapes out of yellow felt. Each hand is two shapes glued together. Leave the wrist ends open so your fingers can fit in.

4. Sew or glue the hands into the open ends of the jogging suit. Fold in the bottom of the jogging suit and sew or glue it.

5. The trousers are two more strips of material – same width, but half the length. Cut a slit in the middle, and fold the edges over into a V-shape. Glue or sew into position.

6. The feet are made the same way as the hands. But you don't leave a gap when you glue them into the bottom of the jogging-suit trousers.

7. The neck is a centimetre-wide strip of cardboard tube from a kitchen roll. Glue or sew the neck into the collar of the jogging suit. Glue the head on top, making sure that the hole you made in the sponge ball is over the neck hole.

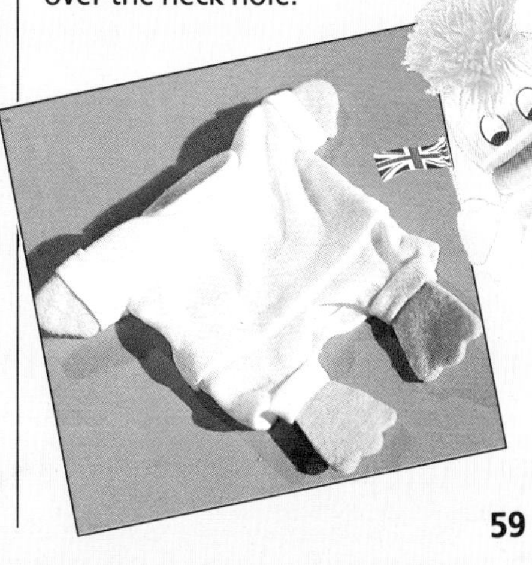

How to win your Blue Peter badge

Be the envy of your friends! Be the envy of your parents (who never managed to win one when they were your age!). Gain entry to a hundred places all over Britain (and one in Holland) absolutely FREE! In other words, win a Blue Peter badge – it's not difficult.

There are five types of badge: Gold, Silver, Blue, Green and Competition. OK, maybe forget about the *Gold*. You will only win that one if you do something extraordinary, like saving someone's life (witnesses needed!) or representing your country. Only a handful are awarded each year.

The most famous Blue Peter badge is the *Blue* badge – the one you see the presenters wearing on the programme. We award them for interesting letters, pictures, poems, recipes, or for good ideas for the programme.

If you've already won a Blue badge, you could win a *Silver* one. We award Silver badges to Blue-badge holders who write to us again. It has to be a different project from the one that won you a Blue badge. So if you sent us a picture before, you could send a recipe or a letter next time.

Green Blue Peter badges started in 1988. We award them for letters, pictures or poems about wildlife or the environment. We love to hear what you are doing to improve your surroundings, or your views on environmental problems.

Competition badges look different from the others. They're awarded to winners and runners-up in our competitions.

When you win your badge, we will send you a list of all the places that give badge-winners free admission. Remember to wear your badge when you visit one!

So get writing – we want to hear from you!

Some useful information...

Blue Peter
BBC TV Centre
London
W12 7RJ

Romanian Orphanage Trust
Fourth Floor
Imperial House
32 Queen Victoria Street
London
EC4N 4SS

Voluntary Service Overseas
317 Putney Bridge Road
London
SW15 2PE

Guide Dogs for the Blind Association
Alexandra House
9 Park Street
Windsor
Berkshire
SL4 1JR

Young Ornithologists' Club
Royal Society for the Protection of Birds
The Lodge
Sandy
Bedfordshire
SG19 2DL

The Hair Book by Anouchka Grose, published by Red Fox, price £3.50

The Royal Ballet
Royal Opera House
Covent Garden
London
WC2E 9DD

The Cresta Run
John Nike Leisure Sports Complex
John Nike Way
Amen Corner
Binfield
Near Bracknell
Berkshire
RG12 4TN
Telephone: 0344 860033

Dinosaurs Alive!
Henry Lowe Associates
2A Weiss Road
London
SW15 1DH
Telephone: 081 789 8864

Euro Tunnel Exhibition Centre
St Martin's Plain
Cheriton High Street
Folkestone
Kent
CT10 4QD
Telephone: 0303 270111

Village Camera by Miss Pinnell and the children of Sapperton School, published by Alan Sutton Publishing, price £13.95

St Tiggywinkle's
The Wildlife Hospital Trust
Aylesbury
Buckinghamshire
Hedgehog Helpline: 0296 29860

The Complete Hedgehog by Les Stocker, published by Chatto & Windus, price £8.99

The Hedgehog and Friends by Les Stocker, published by Chatto & Windus, price £8.99

Did you remember where Yvette's and John's souvenirs came from?

Yvette Fielding (*see p43*)

Yvette's are the baseball she was given by the world-champion Oakland Athletics in San Francisco; the pith helmet she wore in Zimbabwe; and the Tom and Jerry presented to Yvette by Don Messick (the voice of Scrappy Doo) when we filmed at Hanna-Barbera's studios in Los Angeles.

John Leslie (*see p48*)

John's souvenirs are the "Gotcha" Oscar he won on Noel Edmonds' Saturday Roadshow; the Leslie tartan tie; and the steering wheel from the Formula Ford racing car he crashed at Brands Hatch.